T0146536

Medical, Genetic & Behavioral Risk Factors of Bulldogs

By: Ross D. Clark, DVM

H. David Haynes, DVM – Lead Research
and Editorial Assistant
Art J. Quinn, DVM, DACVO – Professor Emeritus,
Oklahoma State University Center
for Veterinary Health Sciences
Brad Howard, DVM – Research Assistant
Paul Schmitz, DVM – Technical Assistant
Jan Coody, MBA – Technical Assistant
Nita Ritschel – Executive Assistant
Geri Hibblen Jackson – Photo Acquisitions
Linda A. Clark, RVT, AKC Judge – Photo Acquisitions

To order additional copies of this book or other breed
books of the 179 AKC recognized breeds by this
author, contact: Xlibris LLC
1-888-795-4274
www.Xlibris.com
Orders@Xlibris.com

MEDICAL, GENETIC & BEHAVIORAL RISK FACTORS OF BULLDOGS

INSIDE:

BY: ROSS D. CLARK, DVM

PREFACE

This book provides you with a through description and positive attributes of this breed including origin, purpose, history, normal heights and weights, acceptable colors and behavioral traits. Our books differ from most books on dog breeds because this book also provides you with a comprehensive and authoritative source of all the known predisposed hereditary health syndromes for the breed. You will find extensive references for each problem described. We also provide the breed club address for this breed and a list of laboratories and organizations that can provide professional help and information.

As a small animal veterinarian, I have always been intrigued by the way dogs have been bred to fill a purpose in life and further impressed that they also tend to love performing that service. Greyhounds and other sight hounds are built for speed with aerodynamic bodies consisting of small head, deep chest, narrow waist and large leg muscles. On the other hand Dachshunds take their name from German words meaning "badger dog" and they use their long nose, long body and short legs to both track, enter and dig into badger dens.

After developing a practice that catered to clients with show dogs, my interest in each breed continued to grow as I studied and observed more and more about the unique predisposition and incidence of health problems in each breed. Breeders of purebred dogs for show were a challenge and inspirational for me to research and help them with their unique health problems. Historically references to hereditary problems are scattered throughout various Veterinary medical texts and journals such as ophthalmology, neurology, gastroenterology, cardiovascular and dermatology. This book, as well as the other books and articles I have written, is researched and compiled with the intention to provide both veterinarians and dog owners with comprehensive and authoritative predisposition information under the breed name.

At the date of this publication, The American Kennel Club Canine Health Foundation and the The Kennel Club of England reports over 400 known hereditary health syndromes throughout the dog kingdom. At the writing of my first book in 1983, less than 50 hereditary issues are able to be predicted and or diagnosed. Sequencing of the canine genome, DNA tests, metabolic testing including blood tests and urine testing; plus, phenotypic examinations such as radiographs, ultrasound, and CERF or OFA eye registry exams by a Board Certified Veterinary Ophthalmologist have advanced the science of breed related health and behavioral problems.

This book will provide veterinarians, researchers, pet owners and breeders with a comprehensive guide to all the known problems veterinarians and dog owners should consider during pet selection and throughout each life stage of our canine friends.

NOTE

The fact that a breed shows many disorders may be more an indication of the extensive research done on that breed than on its comparative soundness of the breed.

Many genetic disorders are common to several breeds. We do not intend to convey severity of incidence by the length of text within a particular breed chapter. One breed may have forty percent incidence and another breed only four percent. If a thorough study has been done to indicate the percentage of incidence, we make note of it; however, please keep in mind the incidence is only an indicator of the dogs tested. A breed for instance may show eighteen percent incidence of hip dysplasia as indicated by OFA, although breeders and veterinarians may not elect to submit radiographs of hips that are so severely dysplastic the owners and their veterinarians know that there is zero chance to be rated as OFA normal.

Please be aware that we have included and identified anecdotal information, defined by Merriam Webster's dictionary as unscientific observation; however, the observations of breeders and veterinarians with a special interest in the breed will hopefully be converted to scientific research, often underwritten by breed clubs, to confirm or rule out predisposition to breed problems.

You will note that each chapter is thoroughly referenced to help with the reader's research as well as to credit and appreciate the researchers, writers, and breeders that have helped the animal world and mankind by their work with these genetic disorders.

Ross D. Clark, D.V.M.

TABLE OF CONTENTS

BULLDOGS

ORIGIN AND HISTORY

The evolutionary history of the Bulldog has been lost. Long ago the breed became a pet and its original function as a bull-baiter was ended. It is believed to have originated in England. Bull refers to the practice of "Bull baiting' and the breed at that time resembled the Staffordshire Bull terrier or Pit Bull terrier. When Bull baiting and dog fighting became illegal in 1835, a program was undertaken to preserve the breed and eliminate its fierce nature. The result is the dog we know today.

The ferocious appearance of the Bulldog belies its calm, friendly temperament. This breed is especially friendly with children.

DESCRIPTION

Today's Bulldogs are shorter, more compact and have more massive heads than their ancestors.

Bulldog jumping in agility

THE SHOW RING

According to the breed Standard, 50 pounds is the ideal weight for males, 40 pounds for bitches. The Bulldogs seen in the show ring are usually slightly heavier. Bulldogs stand between 14 and 17 inches at the shoulders.

The breed Standard allows all colors and mixtures of colors except black. The nose and rims of the eyes should be dark and well-pigmented.

White bulldog

The only breed disqualification is a brown or liver-colored nose.

Bulldog puppies playing

BREEDING AND WHELPING

Because of the short, massive, compact body, accomplishing a tie during breeding is difficult, and frequently the dog and bitch must be held together during mating or artificial insemination must be used.

The gestation period for the Bulldogs is usually 60 days, although in extremely small litters, gestation may exceed 63 days. The average litter size is five.

Bulldog bitches have an unusually hard time whelping.[1,2] Routine cesarean section is recommended for two reasons. First, the dogs have been bred to have large heads and small pelvises, making whelping difficult, and second, since they are a quiescent breed, their muscle tone is poor. Although many bitches can expel one or more puppies, they can rarely sustain the muscle contractions necessary to empty the uterus. An exhausted bitch is a poorer surgical risk for a cesarean section than a bitch that has not been in labor for many hours.

Bulldog family

The birth of 160 litters of Bulldogs was supervised from 1954 to 1957. A bitch that successfully whelped an entire litter without assistance was considered a natural whelper. Only 6% of the observed bitches whelped naturally. This small incidence of natural whelpers is further reason for routine cesarean section.

In the past, a flank incision was recommended for a C section due to the shape of the abdomen and increased visceral pressure on the ventral abdomen. With current advances in suture material, a ventral midline incision is standard procedure today.

RECOGNIZED RISK FACTORS IN BULLDOGS

CARDIOVASCULAR-HEMATOLOGICAL-RESPIRATORY

Anasarca (edematous or Walrus puppies) is a significant problem in the Bulldog. [7] Studies indicate that as many as 8 % of Bulldog puppies delivered by cesarean section are anasarca puppies. A cardio-lymphatic defect is suspected and the condition is believed to be hereditary. Some Bulldog puppies have mild edema of the neck and thorax at birth but unlike anasarca puppies will survive, [8] A **primary peripheral lymphedema** affecting the limbs of adult Bulldogs has been recognized. [31], [34]

Factor VII deficiency and **vonWillebrands disease** [39] have been reported in the Bulldog. Both conditions can result in prolonged bleeding time after surgery or trauma. **Factor VIII** (hemophilia A) has been reported in the breed. The disease is inherited as an X-linked trait with males being affected and females being carriers. Severe factor VIII has been reported resulting in spontaneous bleeding. [43]

The Bulldog is predisposed to several anomalies of the heart that may occur singularly or in groups.

Pulmonic stenosis [31], [32a], occurs in the breed. In the Bulldog, an anomalous coronary artery may compress the right ventricular outflow tract.[33] **Tricuspid valve dysplasia** is seen in Bulldogs with pulmonic stenosis. [33]

Bulldogs are predisposed to **ventricular septal defects.** [26, 27, 28, 31] This condition coupled with pulmonic stenosis results in a right to left shunt.

Aortic stenoses [31] along with **interruption of the aortic arch** [33] and **anomalous subclavian artery** [33] have been reported in Bulldogs. The last condition can compress the esophagus.

The conditions noted above may occur together as **tetralogy of Fallot.** [31]

Bulldogs are predisposed toward **sinus arrhythmias.** [31]

Hereditary laryngeal paralysis has been described in the Bulldog. [39(62)]

Brachycephalic airway syndrome [32b] is most serious in the Bulldog. This condition consisting of stenotic nares, tortuous turbinates, and caudal maxillary displacement with elongated soft palate, everted laryngeal saccules and collapsed tracheal rings compromises the upper airway of the breed. This results in decreased SaO2, increased incidence of sleep-disordered breathing and a predisposition toward heat stroke. All Bulldogs must be intubated when placed under general anesthesia. **Hypoplasia of the trachea** [20] has been reported in this breed.

DERMATOLOGICAL

Bulldogs are predisposed to a form of follicular dysplasia known as **seasonal flank alopecia.** [34] Hair loss begins at 2-4 years of age, and is restricted to the flanks. There is cyclic hair loss and regrowth in some dogs while the alopecia persists in others. Low growth hormone levels found in some affected dogs may implicate hyposomatotropism as a factor but this has yet to be proved. Another condition characterized by bilateral symmetric alopecia and swollen nipples and genitalia in intact females is the result of **hyperestrogenism** usually due to cystic ovaries. [34]

Bulldogs have a predilection for **atopy, demodicosis** and **Malassezia dermatitis.**[12][34]

The wrinkled face and tail conformation of the Bulldog predisposes it for **intertrigo** [34] or skin fold dermatitis. Inflammation is caused by the mechanical rubbing of the skin. This physical characteristic plus their predisposition for atopy account for the increased incidence of pyoderma in the breed. **Folliculitis** and **furunculosis** of the muzzle and facial folds as well as a bacterial **pododermatitis** are common skin infections seen in the Bulldog. [31, 34]

A **dermoid sinus** has been reported in a bulldog. [34] **Mast cell** [19] and **perianal gland tumors** occur in above average numbers in this breed.[34]

ENDOCRINE-EXOCRINE-ENZYMATIC

Bulldogs have a relative high risk for **hypothyroidism.** [29, 34]

GASTROINTESTINAL

Esophageal dilatation caused by compression of the esophagus by an anomalous subclavian artery has been reported in the Bulldog. [32, 33]

The Bulldog is reported to be overrepresented in the incidence of **Hiatal hernia.** [31]

Bulldogs have a predilection for **pyloric stenosis** caused by a congenital hypertrophy of the smooth muscles and are listed as being predisposed toward inflammatory bowel disease. [31]

DENTITION

In proper conformation of the Bulldog's skull, the lower jaw protrudes beyond the upper jaw. The lips must cover the teeth. A **wry mouth** is a major fault. In adult dogs, wry mouths develop due to malocclusion. An extra incisor is often present. [11] The Bulldog is also reported to be at increased risk for dentigerous cysts, a cyst formed from tissue surrounding an unerupted tooth. The mandibular first premolars are most often involved. [31]

MUSCULOSKELETAL

Swimmer puppies are common in the Bulldog. Affected puppies have flat chests and spraddle legs. Since they cannot stand, the pressure of their body weight flattens the cartilaginous portion of the ribs, decreasing chest space and causing labored breathing. These puppies cannot stand at four weeks of age. Treatment includes giving the puppies a rough surface to walk on and taping their rear legs in an adducted position that is at a 90" angle to the plane of the pelvis.

The growing Bulldog is predisposed for **panosteitis**. [46]

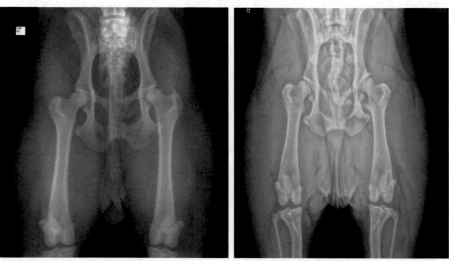

Normal Hips in a Bulldog   Moderate Hip Dysplasia   Source: OFA

Bulldogs are ranked #1 by the OFA in the incidence of **hip dysplasia** with 72.0% of the films evaluated being abnormal.[37] There is also an increased incidence of **patellar luxation** in this breed. [23, 37]

Bulldogs are classified as an **achondroplastic** breed. This is an incomplete autosomal dominant trait that causes failure of cartilage growth and delayed endochondral ossification. The forelimbs are most affected with limb shortening and flared metaphyses. The limb is predisposed to **shoulder joint laxity** and **elbow dysplasia**. [21, .23, 31] 36.5% of the elbow evaluations submitted to the OFA were abnormal. [37] Abnormalities can also occur in the vertebrae and the breed is at increased risk for **Osteochondrosis of the stifle**. [46]

Craniomandibular osteopathy has been reported in the breed. [31]

NEUROLOGICAL

Deafness [30, 31] and **hydrocephalus** [15, 31] have been reported to occur in Bulldogs.

Achondroplasia in the Bulldog can result in vertebral and spinal cord abnormalities: **Hemivertebra** [15, 24, 25, 35] (incomplete ossification of the vertebral body), **spina bifida** (incomplete closure of the dorsal vertebral arch), [9, 35] and **sacrocaudal dysgenesis**. [31, 39(1028)] Spinal cord anomalies include myelochisis, meningocele and myelomeningocele. Clinical signs vary based on the degree of spinal cord involvement. In Bulldogs, there is often dysfunction of the areas served by the cauda equina. [35] Knecht has reported **stenosis of the thoracic spinal canal** in the breed. [38]

Idiopathic head tremors have been reported in Bulldogs. [31]

Cerebellar degeneration has been reported in three related Bulldogs. All three dogs were presented with progressive cerebellar dysfunction: hypermetria, spasticity, tremors and loss of balance. Lesions were confined to the cerebellar cortex with loss of Purkinje and granule cells. [45]

Diskospondylitis is an infection of the vertebral column affecting the cartilaginous vertebral endplates with secondary involvement of the disks. Staphylococcus aureus is the most frequently reported infectious agent. It is spread via the blood from other locations such as abscesses and oral infections. Clinical signs are non-specific early on and include a malaise, anorexia and vertebral pain. Vertebral instability, luxation and neurologic deficits may occur later. A recent study indicated that the Bulldog was at 3 times greater risk for diskospondylitis than the general population. [40]

OPHTHALMIC

Eury/Macroblepharon is defined as an exceptionally large palpebral fissure and is found in the Bulldog. This condition can lead to lower lid Ectropion and upper lid Entropion both of which can cause ocular irritation. [36]

Entropion and **ectropion** are found in the Bulldog; as are **distichiasis** (eyelashes abnormally located on the eyelid margin) and **ectopic cilia** (hair emerging through the eyelid conjunctiva). [31, 36]

Bulldogs have an increased incidence of **prolapse of the gland of the third eyelid** (Cherry eye). [36]

Nonulcerative keratitis and **keratoconjunctivitis sicca** [14, 31, 36] are seen in Bulldogs. Facial fold irritation may be responsible for the first condition while the second is due to a tear film abnormality with immune-mediated destruction of the tear glands. **Chronic superficial keratitis (Pannus)** has also been recognized in the breed. The condition begins as a grayish haze in the ventral or ventrolateral cornea. Vascularization and pigmentation follow as the lesion moves toward the central cornea. [36]

Cataracts are found in this breed. [36]

Bulldogs have a predisposition for **retinal dysplasia** (Folds). [36] Triangular, curved or curvilinear folds are seen in the retina of Bulldog puppies. These folds may resolve with maturity. They do not appear to affect vision.

UROGENITAL

Bulldogs have such a high incidence of **dystocia** [1,2,31] that scheduled cesarean sections are the rule rather than the exception.

A higher than average incidence of **cryptorchidism** has been reported in the Bulldog. [6]

Young female Bulldogs are one of the breeds predisposed for **vaginal hyperplasia** and **prolapse**. [31] Male Bulldogs between the age of 9 and 13 months have an increased incidence of **urethral prolapse**. [22, 31]

Female Bulldogs are predisposed for **ectopic ureters**. [10, 31]

Cystinuria and **cystine uroliths** occur in the Bulldog. This is caused by a metabolic defect in which Cystine is inadequately reabsorbed by the proximal tubules. Cystinuria dogs may or may not form uroliths.

Bulldogs have a breed predilection for **hyperuricosuria**, elevated levels of uric acid in the urine. This predisposed the affected dogs for **urate uroliths** due to impaired conversion of uric acid. [31] The condition is inherited as an autosomal recessive trait. A mutation in exon 5 of the gene Solute carrier family2, member 9 (SLC2A9) has been found to be responsible for hyperuricosuria in the dog. The University of California, Davis Veterinary Genetics Lab offers a DNA test for this condition. [42]

BEHAVIOR

The Bulldog is treasured as a family dog. He is good-natured, conservative, dignified and loyal. He is clean but he is a drooler. Surveys conducted in Germany, Japan and the USA rank the Bulldog low in reactivity (activity, excitability, affection and playfulness), slightly above average in owner dominance and average in dog aggression. The breed was generally ranked low in trainability. [47, 48, 49]

OLD AGE

The average life span of this breed is from 8 to 10 years, although some dogs live to 14 years of age. A survey of the Veterinary Medical Database indicated that cancer was the most often diagnosed cause of death in the Bulldog with congenital defects in second place. Cardiac and respiratory system failures were also frequent. [44]

MISCELLANEOUS

Bulldogs have a higher than average incidence of **Sjögren's syndrome**. [31] Significant features of this autoimmune disease include keratoconjunctivitis sicca, xerostomia and lymphoplasmacytic adenitis. It develops concurrently with other immune-mediated diseases.

Bulldogs are predisposed toward **lymphosarcoma**. [16, 17, 18, 31, and 34]

MISCELLANEOUS FACTS AND RESOURCES

This is a list of Genetic tests available for Bulldogs to identify inherited medical problems that may be recommended by your Veterinarian

Condition   Laboratory

Hyperuricosuria   UC Davis Veterinary Genetics Lab, VetGen, Animal Health Trust, UK
For information about the laboratories performing these tests and sample submission contact:
www.offa.org/dna_labs.html

Additional health screening tests recommended for Bulldogs by the Canine Health Information Center (CHIC)

Here is how CHIC works to help dog fanciers improve their breeds

CHIC works with national breed clubs, the AKC Canine Health Foundation and the Orthopedic Foundation for Animals (OFA) to create a list of health screening procedures designed to eliminate inherited health problems from dogs used for breeding. The procedures vary from breed to breed and may change if new problems are identified or new tests become available. A dog must have completed all the required health screening procedures in order to receive a CHIC number. For more information contact: www.caninehealthinfo.org/

CHIC REQUIREMENTS FOR BULLDOGS

Patellar Luxation: OFA evaluation, minimum age one year
Congenital Cardiac Database: OFA evaluation, exam by a Boarded Cardiologist using echocardiography is preferred but not required.
Tracheal Hypoplasia: OFA radiographic evaluation for tracheal hypoplasia.
Eye Exam by a boarded ACVO Ophthalmologist (Optional): After the age of 24 months with results registered with CERF or OFA
Hip Dysplasia (Optional): OFA evaluation
Elbow Dysplasia (Optional): OFA evaluation
Autoimmune Thyroiditis (Optional): OFA evaluation from an approved laboratory
Congenital Deafness (Optional): OFA evaluation based on BAER test
Hyperuricosuria (Optional): DNA test from the UC Davis Veterinary Genetics Lab [41]

NATIONAL BREED CLUB

The National Breed Club is a good place to discover all the things you can do with your Bulldog and to contact other Bulldog owners.

BULLDOG CLUB OF AMERICA

www.bullddogclubofamerica.org

REFERENCES

1. Freak, M.J. "The Whelping Bitch," Vet. Rec; 1947: 60: 295-301.
2. Freak, M.J. "Abnormal Conditions Associated with Pregnancy and Parturition in the Bitch," Vet. Rec.; 1962: 74: 1323-1335.
3. Kirk, R.W. and Bistner, S.I. Handbook of Veterinary Procedures and Emergency Treatment: Hereditary Defects of Dogs; 1975: Table 124; 661.
4. Hutt, F.B. "Inherited Lethal Characteristics in Domestic Animals," Cornell Vet; 1934: 2. 1-25.
5. Pearce, R.C. "Anomalies of the English Bulldog," Southwest Vet J.; 1969: 22:218-220.
6. Bell, Jerold S. DVM "Sex Related Genetic Disorders: Did Mama Cause Them?" American Kennel Club Gazette, Feb. 1994; 76.
7. Ladds, P.W., Dennis, S.M., Leipold, H.W. "Lethal Congenital Edema in Bulldog Pups," JAVMA; 1971: 159:81-86.
8. Stockard, C.R. "The Genetic and Endocrine Basis for Differences in Form and Behavior As Elucidated by Studies of Contrasted Pure-Line Dog Breeds and Hybrids," Am. Anat. Mem.; Wistar Institute of Anatomy and Biology.
9. Curtis, R.L., English, D. and Kim, Y.J. "Spinal Bifida in a Stub Dog Stock: Selectively Bred for Short Tails," Anat. Ret; 1964: 148:365.
10. Hayes, H.M., Jr., "Breed Association of Canine Ectopic Ureter: A Study of 217 Female Cases," J. Sm. Aim. Prac; 1984: 258, 501504; 12 ref.
11. Aitchison, J. "Incisor Dentition in Short Muzzled Dogs," Vet. Rec; 1964: 76:165-1 69.
12. Griffin, C., Kowchka, K., McDonald, J.; Current Veterinary Dermatology, the Science and Art of Therapy. Mosby Yearbook, St. Louis, MO 1993: 74, 101.
13. Magrane, W.G. Canine Ophthalmology; (3rd ed. Lea & Febiger, Philadelphia, PA 1977) 305.
14. Pearce, Richard C. DVM, Bulldog Column, American Kennel Club Gazette; 119, December, 1991.
15. Erickson, F., Saperstein, G., Leipold, H.W. et al, "Congenital Defects of Dogs Ill," Canine Practice; 1977: 4(6): 48.
16. Madewell, Bruce R., VMD, MS., "Canine Lymphoma," Veterinarian Clinics of North American Small Animal Practice; July, 1985: Vol. 15, #4.
17. McCaw, Dudley, DVM, "Canine Lymphosarcoma," AAHA's 56th Annual Meeting Proceedings, 1989.
18. Rosenthal, Robert C., DVM, MS, PhD. "The Treatment of Multicentric Canine Lymphoma," Veterinarian Clinics of North America Small Animal Practice; July, 1990: Vol 20, #4.
19. Veterinary News, The American Kennel Club Gazette; April, 1990: 44.
20. Suter, P.F., Cosgrove, D.J. and Ewing, G.O. "Congenital Hypoplasia of the Canine Trachea," JAAHA; 1972: 8:120-1 27.
21. Bodner, Elizabeth, DVM. "Genetic Status Symbols," The American Kennel Club Gazette; September, 1992.
22. Sinibaldi, K.R. and Green, R.W. "Surgical Correction of Prolapse of the Male Urethra in Three English Bulldogs," JAAHA; 1973: 9: 450-453.
23. Ettinger, S.J.; Textbook of Veterinary Internal Medicine. W.B. Saunders, Philadelphia, PA. 1989: 2283.
24. Done, S.H., Drew, R.A., Robins, G.M., Lane, J.G. "Hemivertebra in the Dog: Clinical and Pathological Observations," Vet. Rec.; 1975: 96: 313-317.
25. Drew, R.A. "Possible Association Between Vertebral Development and Neonatal Mortality in Bulldogs," Vet. Rec.; 1974: 94: 480-481.
26. Mulvihill, J.J. and Priester, W.A. "Congenital Heart Disease in Dogs, Epidemiologic Similarities in Man," Teratology; 1973: 7: 73-78.
27. Patterson, D.F. "Epidemiologic and Genetic Studies of Congenital Heart Disease in the Dog," Circulation Research; 1968: 23: 171-202.
28. Patterson, D.F. "Canine Congenital Heart Disease, Epidemiological Hypotheses," J. Sm. Aim. Prac; 1971: 12:263-287.
29 Brignac, Michele M. "Congenital and Breed Associated Skin Diseases in the Dog and Cat," KalKan

Forum; December, 1989: 9-16.

30. Strain, George M. "Deafness in Dogs and Cats," Proc. 70th ACVIM; May, 1992.

31. Tilley, Lawrence P., Smith, Francis W.K. Jr. the 5 Minute Veterinary Consult; Canine and Feline, 4th ed. Ames, IA, Blackwell Publishing 2007

32a. Thomas, William P., Therapy of Congenital Pulmonic Stenosis

32b. Hendricks, Joan C., Recognition and Treatment of Congenital Respiratory Tract Defects in Brachycephalics

32c. Guilford, W. Grant, Breed-Associated Gastrointestinal Disease, Kirk's Current Veterinary Therapy XII Philadelphia, PA; W.B. Saunders Co. 1995

33. Kittleson, Mark D., Kienle, Richard D. Small Animal Cardiovascular Medicine. St. Louis, MO; Mosby Inc. 1998

34. Scott, Danny W., Miller, William H. Jr., Griffin, Craig E. Muller and Kirk's Small Animal dermatology- 5th ed. Philadelphia, PA; W.B. Saunders Co. 2001

35. Oliver, John E. Jr., Lorenz, Michael D., Korngay, Joe N. Handbook of Veterinary Neurology, 3rd. ed. Philadelphia, PA; W.B. Saunders Co. 1997

36. Genetics Committee of the American College of Veterinary Ophthalmologists; Ocular Disorders Presumed to be Inherited in Purebred Dogs. 5th ed. 2009

37. Orthopedic Foundation for Animals website: www.offa.org

38. Knecht C., Blevens, W.E., Raffe, M.R. Stenosis of the thoracic spinal canal in English Bulldogs J. Am Ani Hosp. Assoc. 15:182-182, 1979

39. Ackerman, Lowell. The Genetic Connection: A Guide to Health Problems in Purebred Dogs. Lakewood, CO: AAHA Press, 1999

40. Burkert, Blaine A., Kerwin, Sharon C. et. al. Signalment and clinical features of diskospondylitis in dogs: 513 cases (1980-2001). JAVMA, Vol. 227, No. 2, July 15, 2005. p. 268-74

41. Bulldog-Breeds Requirements, CHIC Breeds, Canine Health Information Center: www.caninehealthinfo. org

42. Canine Hyperuricosuria UC Davis Veterinary Genetics Laboratory website: www.vgl.ucdavis.edu/ services/Hyperuricosuria.php

43. Brooks, M. A Review of Canine Inherited Bleeding Disorders: Biochemical and Molecular Strategies for Disease Characterization and Carrier Detection; The Journal of Heredity 90(1) 1999

44. Fleming, J.M., Creevy, K.E., Promislow, D.E.L. Mortality in North American Dogs from 1984 to 2004: an Investigation into Age-, Size-, and Breed-Related Causes of Death Journal of Veterinary Internal Medicine Vol. 25, Issue 2 March/April 2011 pages 187-198

45. Gandini, G., Botterton, C., Brini, E. Et Al Cerebellar cortical degeneration in three English bulldogs: Clinical and neuropathological findings. Journal of Small Animal Practice 2005 Jun; 46(6):291-4

46. LaFond, E., Breur, G.J., Austin, C.C. Breed susceptibility for developmental orthopedic diseases in dogs. J. Am Anim Hosp Assoc, 2002; 38:467-77

47. Takeuchi, Y. Mori, Y. A Comparison of the Behavioral Profiles of Purebred Dogs in Japan to Profiles of those in the United States and the United Kingdom J Vet Med Sci 68 789-90 2006

48. Turcsan, B., Kubinyi, E. Miklosi, A. Trainability and boldness traits differ between dog breed clusters based on conventional breed categories and genetic relatedness Appl Anim Behav Sci 2011 132:61-70

49. Hart, B.L., Hart, L. The Perfect Puppy, How to Choose Your Dog by Its Behavior New York, Barnes & Noble Books, 2001

Printed in the United States
By Bookmasters